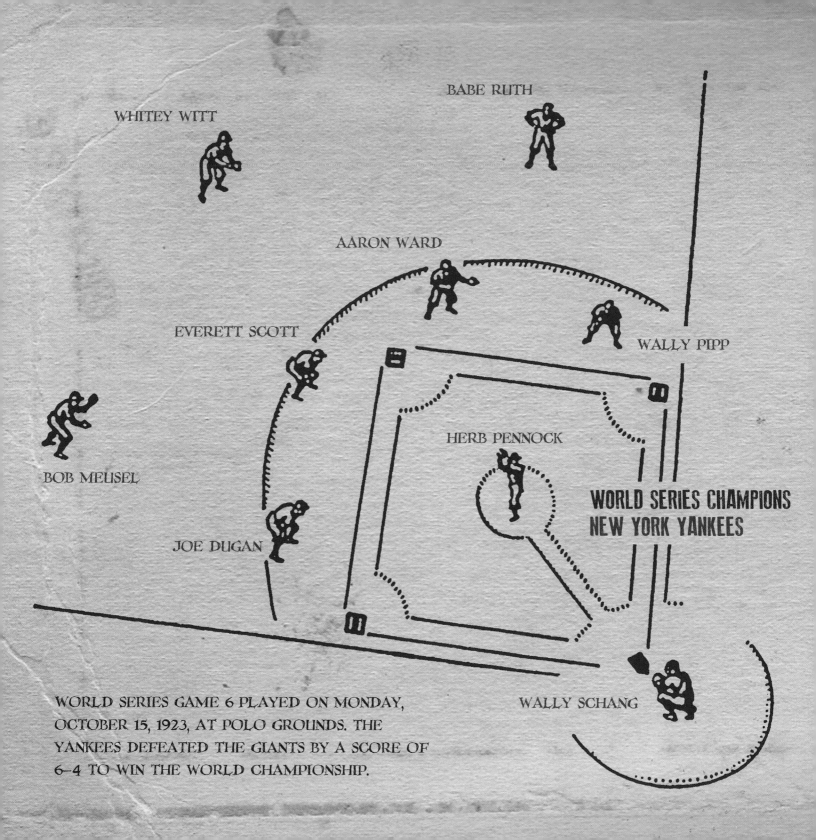

WHITEY WITT

BABE RUTH

AARON WARD

EVERETT SCOTT

WALLY PIPP

BOB MEUSEL

HERB PENNOCK

WORLD SERIES CHAMPIONS
NEW YORK YANKEES

JOE DUGAN

WALLY SCHANG

WORLD SERIES GAME 6 PLAYED ON MONDAY,
OCTOBER 15, 1923, AT POLO GROUNDS. THE
YANKEES DEFEATED THE GIANTS BY A SCORE OF
6–4 TO WIN THE WORLD CHAMPIONSHIP.

NEW YORK YANKEES

SARA GILBERT

CREATIVE EDUCATION

Published by Creative Education
P.O. Box 227, Mankato, Minnesota 56002
Creative Education is an imprint of The Creative Company
www.thecreativecompany.us

Design and production by Blue Design (www.bluedes.com)
Art direction by Rita Marshall
Printed in the United States of America

Photographs by Getty Images (Ron Antonelli/NY Daily News
Archive, Al Bello, Ryan D. Budhu, Diamond Images, Focus on
Sport, Charles Franklin/MLB Photos, Leon Halip, Jed Jacobsohn/
Allsport, Keystone, Kidwiler Collection/Diamond Images, Edwin
Levick/Hulton Archive, Jim McIsaac, National Baseball Hall of
Fame Library/MLB Photos, NY Daily News Archive, Hy Peskin/
Time & Life Pictures, Rich Pilling/MLB Photos, Photo File/MLB
Photos, Arthur Rickerby/Diamond Images, Robert Riger, Mark
Rucker/Transcendental Graphics, Jamie Squire, Mike Theiler/AFP)

Library of Congress Cataloging-in-Publication Data
Gilbert, Sara.
New York Yankees / Sara Gilbert.
p. cm. — (World series champions)
Includes bibliographical references and index.
Summary: A simple introduction to the New York Yankees major
league baseball team, including its start in 1903, its World Series
triumphs, and its stars throughout the years.
ISBN 978-1-60818-269-5
1. New York Yankees (Baseball team)—History—Juvenile literature.
I. Title.
GV875.N4G54 2013
796.357'64097471—dc23   2012004263

First edition
9 8 7 6 5 4 3 2 1

Cover: Pitcher C. C. Sabathia
Page 2: Center fielder Mickey Mantle
Page 3: Left fielder Hideki Matsui
Right: Second baseman Robinson Cano

CF JOE DiMAGGIO

C THURMAN MUNSON

SS BUCKY DENT

RF ROGER MARIS

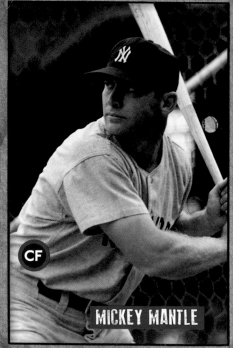
CF MICKEY MANTLE

P JACK CHESBRO

TABLE OF CONTENTS

NEW YORK AND YANKEE STADIUM

New York City is a huge city in New York. It is the largest city in the United States. New York is home to Yankee Stadium, where the Yankees baseball team plays its home games.

RIVALS AND COLORS

The Yankees play major league baseball. They try to win the World Series to become world champions. The Yankees wear white-and-black uniforms. Their fiercest **RIVALS** are the Boston Red Sox.

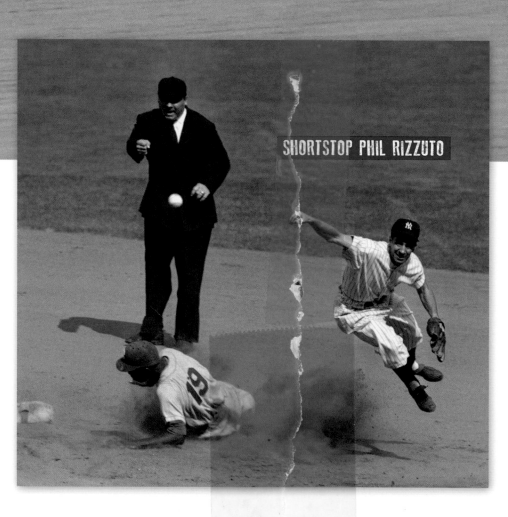

SHORTSTOP PHIL RIZZUTO

PITCHER C. C. SABATHIA

YANKEES HISTORY

New York's first season was in 1901. The Yankees got off to a slow start. They did not make the **PLAYOFFS** until 1921. Outfielder Babe Ruth slugged a lot of home runs to help the Yankees reach the World Series many times in the years after that. They won the championship three times in the 1920s.

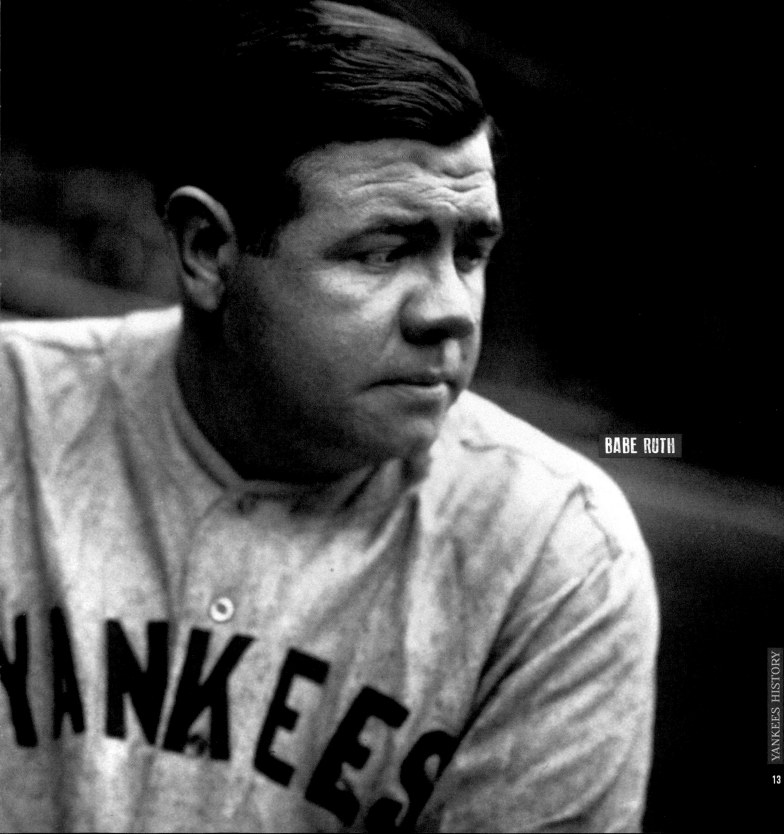

BABE RUTH

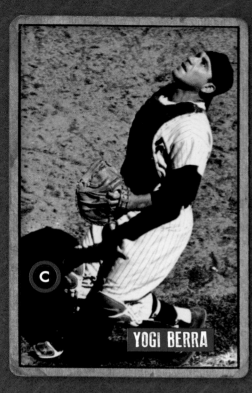

C

YOGI BERRA

1B

TINO MARTINEZ

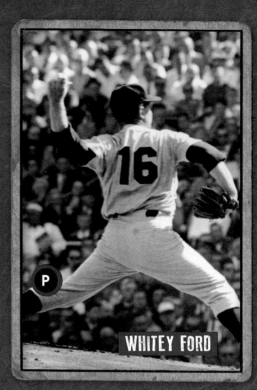

P

WHITEY FORD

1B

LOU GEHRIG

3B

GRAIG NETTLES

P

MARIANO RIVERA

JOE DiMAGGIO

VERSATILE outfielder Joe DiMaggio led the Yankees to four straight world championships from 1936 to 1939. The Yankees won five more World Series from 1949 to 1953. By 1963, New York had 20 trophies!

REGGIE JACKSON

Powerful outfielder Reggie Jackson helped New York capture championships in 1977 and 1978. Then the Yankees went into a **SLUMP**. They missed the playoffs every year for a long time.

With new manager Joe Torre, the Yankees got better in 1996. They made the playoffs for 13 straight years. By 2011, they had won four more world championships.

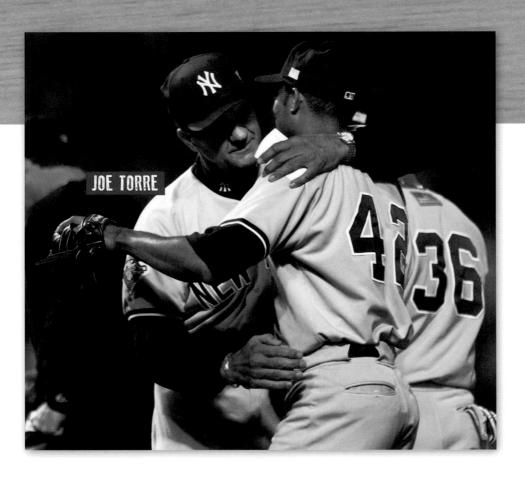

JOE TORRE

DON MATTINGLY

LOU GEHRIG

YANKEES STARS

From 1925 to 1939, first baseman Lou Gehrig played in 2,130 straight games. Fans called him "The Iron Horse." Outfielder Mickey Mantle joined the Yankees in 1951. He bashed 536 home runs for New York.

Don Mattingly was a fan favorite in New York from 1982 to 1995. He always played hard. In 1996, shortstop Derek Jeter became

New York's newest star. He hit the ball hard and was a great fielder, too.

First baseman Mark Teixeira slammed many home runs starting in 2009. He helped the Yankees win their 27th world championship that year. New York fans hoped Teixeira and the Yankees would win more trophies soon!

MARK TEIXEIRA

DEREK JETER

HOW THE YANKEES GOT THEIR NAME

The Yankees were called the Highlanders at first because their home field was on top of a hill. But that name was too long to use for headlines in newspapers. Sportswriters started calling them Yankees instead. "Yankees" is a word that describes people who live in and around New York.

ABOUT THE YANKEES

First season: 1901

League/division: American League, East Division

World Series championships:

1923	4 games to 2 versus New York Giants
1927	4 games to 0 versus Pittsburgh Pirates
1928	4 games to 0 versus St. Louis Cardinals
1932	4 games to 0 versus Chicago Cubs
1936	4 games to 2 versus New York Giants
1937	4 games to 1 versus New York Giants
1938	4 games to 0 versus Chicago Cubs
1939	4 games to 0 versus Cincinnati Reds
1941	4 games to 1 versus Brooklyn Dodgers
1943	4 games to 1 versus St. Louis Cardinals
1947	4 games to 3 versus Brooklyn Dodgers

1949   4 games to 1 versus Brooklyn Dodgers
1950   4 games to 0 versus Philadelphia Phillies
1951   4 games to 2 versus New York Giants
1952   4 games to 3 versus Brooklyn Dodgers
1953   4 games to 2 versus Brooklyn Dodgers
1956   4 games to 3 versus Brooklyn Dodgers
1958   4 games to 3 versus Milwaukee Braves
1961   4 games to 1 versus Cincinnati Reds
1962   4 games to 3 versus San Francisco Giants
1977   4 games to 2 versus Los Angeles Dodgers
1978   4 games to 2 versus Los Angeles Dodgers
1996   4 games to 2 versus Atlanta Braves
1998   4 games to 0 versus San Diego Padres
1999   4 games to 0 versus Atlanta Braves
2000   4 games to 1 versus New York Mets
2009   4 games to 2 versus Philadelphia Phillies

Yankees Web site for kids:

http://mlb.mlb.com/nyy/fan_forum/kids_index.jsp

Club MLB:

http://web.clubmlb.com/index.html

GLOSSARY

PLAYOFFS — all the games (including the World Series) after the regular season that are played to decide who the champion will be

RIVALS — teams that play extra hard against each other

SLUMP — a period of time when a team loses more games than it wins

VERSATILE — able to do many different things well

INDEX